Lend Me Your Ears
Telephone Jokes

Compiled by Charles Keller
Illustrated by Dana Fradon

PIPPIN PRESS
New York

For Gabe

Published by Pippin Press, 229 East 85th Street,
Gracie Station Box #1347, New York, N.Y. 10028

10 9 8 7 6 5 4 3 2 1

Library of Congress Cataloging-in-Publication Data

Lend me your ears : compiled by Charles Keller :
    illustrated by Dana Fradon.
        p.   cm.

    Summary: A collection of jokes and riddles
about the telephone, including "Where do sea
creatures buy their mobile phones? At Radio
Shark."
    ISBN 0-945912-23-4
    1. Telephone—Juvenile humor.   2. Riddles,
Juvenile.   I. Keller,
Charles.   II. Fradon, Dana, Ill.
PN6231.T5L46   1994
818'.540208—dc20   94-7031
                                                            CIP
                                                            AC

Hello, is Len there?
Len who?
Len me your ears.

How will messages travel on the new telecommunications highway?
In-formation.

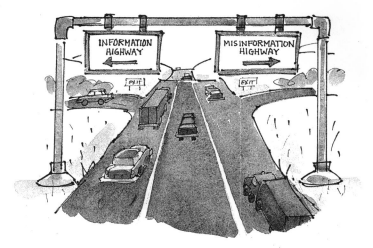

Hello, 911.

I'd like to report a missing dog.

This number is for emergencies only.

But, my dog is very intelligent. He can talk.

Then you'd better hang up. He may be trying to call you.

I have an odd sound in my ear—like a phone ringing.

Well, why don't you pick it up?

I hope everyone read the science assignment and didn't waste time talking on the phone all evening. Joan, what can you tell me about nitrates?

They're cheaper than day rates.

Hello, how would you like a device that can stop you from receiving annoying phone calls?
I already have one—my finger—"click."

What phone service is found in restaurants?
B.L.T. & T.

What were Alexander Graham Bell's first words?
"Goo, goo."

How can you tell when you're getting on the information highway?
You're asked to pay a toll call.

Why did the person sit by the phone for hours?
He was trying out "call waiting."

I removed my "call waiting" and put in call backwards.
Why?
It lets me talk to myself.

What do you get when you cross a pair of roller blades, a fax machine and a beeper?
A new sport called roller-paging.

What happens when you call a bee?
You get a buzzy signal.

What's the most popular phone at a gas station?
The Mobil phone.

What do historians talk about on the phone?
Old times.

Little girl, would you take a message for me?
Okay.
Tell your father to call me at Capital 5-1212.
Okay, but how do you make a capital "5"?

What did the mother phone say when she scolded the kid phone?
"Don't speak to me in that tone."

What did the duck say when he made a charge call?
"Just put it on my bill."

What was wrong with the counterfeit phone?
It was phoney.

What does the Roadrunner's answering-machine message say?
"Please leave your name and number after the BEEP, BEEP."

Why did the phone see the psychiatrist?
It had a big hang-up.

What was the earliest form of long distance communication?
The Phoney Express.

What snacks do people eat on the information highway?
Cracker Fax.

What do you get when you cross a sink and a telephone?
A phone tap.

Why was the writer confused by his fax machine?
Because he couldn't tell fax from fiction.

Why are telephone rates so high in Iran?
Everyone is speaking Persian to Persian.

What did the Hollywood star get when she dropped her cellular phone into the hot tub?
Call wading.

Which company has the best "fast forwarding"?
Sprint.

Do you have a phone book?
No, I'll wait to see the movie.

Hello, mental health call-in show. My aunt is a kleptomaniac. What should I do?
Is she taking anything for it?

Why was the car phone late for the meeting?
It got hung up in traffic.

What football position does the telephone play?
Receiver.

What do you call a phone at a grocery store?
Telemarketing.

I've developed a bad habit of making long-distance calls to myself.
That could be expensive.
Not really. I always reverse the charges.

Why is waiting on the telephone like a trapeze act?
Because you have to hang on.

What's yellow and seldom rings?
An unlisted banana.

What do you call fear of talking into small, plastic objects?
Telephobia.

Why did the telephone cross the road?
To make a short-distance call.

Who invented the telephone and had a cookie named after him?
Alexander Graham Cracker.

What happens when a human body is submerged in water?
The telephone rings.

I've come to fix the phone.
You should have come yesterday.
I called five times and got no answer.

How can you tell how old a telephone is?
You count the rings.

Why is it useless to call Washington?
Because he's dead.

I hear they're putting fax machines in cars.
Why?
If you are speeding, instead of pulling you over, the cops fax you the ticket.

Who invented the telephone?
The Phoe-nicians.

What is old McDonald's area code?
E-I-E-I-O.

What's cheap talk?
A local phone call.

Doctor, I hate to bother you at 3 A.M., but I have a bad case of insomnia.
Well, what are you trying to do, start an epidemic?

What kind of phone makes music?
The saxophone.

What do you call dirty windows on phone booths?
Stained glass.

I'm saving my money to buy one of those new Japanese cellular phones.
But how will you know what they are saying?

What do telephones do on January first?
They ring in the New Year.

What do you call an ox that talks a lot?
A yakety yak.

What do you do if you get a ringing in your ear?
Get an unlisted ear.

What is the best color for a car phone?
Yello.

Who first said, "Talk is cheap."?
Someone who didn't have to pay the phone bill.

Why don't you answer the phone?
Because it isn't ringing.
Must you always wait until the last minute?

What would you have if plants had telephones?
Interplantetary communications.

Fire department! Come quickly! My garage is on fire!
How do we get there?
Don't you still have that red truck?

Didn't the phone just ring?
Yes, it was the operator. She said, "It's long distance from Los Angeles," and I said, "Yes it is," and hung up.

What kind of phone call is it when one preacher talks to another preacher?
Parson to parson.

How can you tell when you've reached a number in Tibet?
Everyone is saying "yak, yak, yak."

Why did the telephone company disconnect the chicken's phone?
He was using fowl language.

Do you believe in free speech?
Why, of course.
Good. Mind if I use your phone?

Hello, advice call-in show. Is it true that you can catch more flies with honey than with vinegar?
Sure, but who wants a lot of flies?

What's the perfect gift for someone in prison?
A cell-ular phone.

What do you call a telephone on wheels?
A mobile phone.

What's a telephone's favorite soap?
Dial.

What do you call a phone company in Mexico?
Taco Bell.

What do you get when a shark talks on the phone?

A fish that talks your ear off.

How do scientists in different countries send data to each other?

They fax the facts.

In what language do telephone operators speak?

A dial-ect.

Airline information.
How long does it take to fly from New York to San Francisco?
Just a minute.
Thank you.

Why is it hard to talk on the phone with a goat around?
Because it always butts in.

You say Mary is sick and can't come to school. Who is this speaking?
This is my mother.

Madam, your phone doesn't work because it has a short circuit.
Okay, then lengthen it.

What ring is connected to a phone?
An answer-ring machine.

What flowers grow near a telephone mouthpiece?
Tulips.

What's a telephone booth?
A chat in the box.

Can you come to my house and play?
I have to take a bath and do my homework before I'm allowed out.
How long will it take?
Give me five minutes.

What's the best way to talk to a shark?
Long distance.

Will you please come over to fix my car? I flooded the carburetor.

Okay, where is it now?

At the bottom of the swimming pool.

Can astronauts telephone from the space shuttle?

Sure. Who can't tell a phone from a space shuttle.

You usually talk on the phone for an hour. But you hung up after a half hour. How come?
Wrong number.

Hello, advice call-in show. What's the best way to keep my phone bill down?
Use a heavy paperweight.

What's the most popular phone company in outer space?
E.T. & T.

Hello, First National Bank.
I'd like to borrow some money.
I'm sorry but the loan arranger isn't in today.
Okay, then let me speak to Tonto.

What never gets asked a question but always gives an answer?
An answering machine.

How does a cat use a telephone?
He talks into the mousepiece.

Where do telephone talkers get their reading material?
The Book-of-the-Mouth Club.

What do you call a marriage of two telephone operators in California?
A western union.

Why couldn't Tarzan get Jane on the phone?
Her vine was busy.

We have a phone in our car.
That's nothing. We have a car pool.

What do you call a person who sells mobile phones for cars?
A wheeler dealer.

Why did the football players cram into the phone booth?
They were trying to get the quarterback.

How come your teenage daughter doesn't say anything?
She's not used to talking until she hears the dial tone.

Doctor, I feel as though I'm a horse.
Come in to see me. I think I can cure you. But it will cost a lot of money.
Money is no problem. I just won the Kentucky Derby.

Where do sea creatures buy their mobile phones?
At Radio Shark.

What did the sheep's daughter say to her mother when she answered the phone?
"It's for ewe."

Why should your fax machine be on a level surface?
To get the fax straight.

Why do cows talk on mobile phones?
To cow-moo-nicate.

How do polar bears send their mail?
They use the bear fax.

Hello, is this the talk-show host? Why are your listeners always complaining about the high cost of living? My wife and I live on two dollars a week.

Two dollars! That's incredible! I want to hear how you do it. Could you speak a little louder so our listeners can hear.

I can't speak louder. I'm a goldfish.

Mister, could you lend me a quarter? I need to call home. It's an emergency.

Are you homesick?

No, I'm here sick.

Hello, this is the electric company. Is your refrigerator running?

Yes, it is.

Well, you'd better run and catch it.

Hello, science call-in show.

Why doesn't lightning strike twice in the same place?

After the first time, the place isn't there any more.

Do you ever hear voices without being able to tell who's talking or where the voices are coming from?

Yes, as a matter of fact I do.

When does this happen?

When I answer the phone.

Why did the spy spray insect repellent on the phone?
To keep it from being bugged.

Hello, little girl, this is the police chief. Are any of my officers there?
No, they're not.
Well, is your mother or father there?
No, they're all out looking for me.

How can you tell an African elephant from an Indian elephant?
They have different area codes.

Mom, I bought this sweater for twenty-five dollars. Isn't it a bargain?
Why didn't you call me first?
What! And waste a quarter?

When my son calls home from college he calls me, "Darling." What does yours call you?
He calls me collect.

What do you get when you cross a crab with an answering machine?
A snappy answer.

IT'S FOR YOU.

Why do bird-watchers carry mobile phones?
To practice their bird calls.

What do you hear when a cow puts you on hold?
Moo-sic.

Sorry, but you have the wrong number.
Are you sure?
Have I ever lied to you before?

What's the difference between a fax machine and the flu?
One makes facsimiles and the other makes sick families.

I'm having trouble with my fax machine.
What's the problem?
When I turn it on it flashes ENTER and I can't find the door.

What did the president say when he picked up the hot line?
"Ouch!"

Why did the cowboy whisper on the mobile phone?
He had bronc-itis.

I have bad news for you and I have worse news for you.
What's the bad news, doc?
You only have forty-eight hours to live.
Forty-eight hours! What could be worse than that?
I've been trying to reach you for two days.

What do you call an expensive car phone?
A Rolls Voice.

Why did the woman turn her back to the phone?
She didn't want to face the fax.

What did the insect order from the phone company?
An ant-swering machine and a bee-per.

Hello, health call-in show. Is the water in my town healthy?
Yes, they only use well water.

What's the hardest part of Superman's job?
Remembering which phone booth he left his clothes in.

What do angels say when they answer the phone?
"Halo."